Note To Parents And Readers

This is a story about colors and some of the different ways to say them.

Wherever an individual color is presented, the large words on the right side of the page will show how that color is spoken, always in the same order and in the following languages:

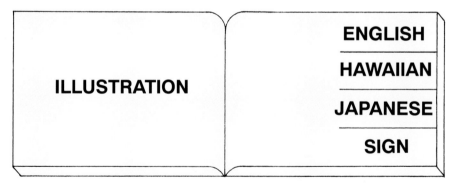

ILLUSTRATION

ENGLISH

HAWAIIAN

JAPANESE

SIGN

At the end of the story is a glossary and a pronunciation guide which may be helpful.

When using sign language, use your hands or fingers to follow the direction arrows if they are shown, and say the words you are signing.

We hope you enjoy the story.

Dedicated to the beautiful children of Hawaii.

Published by Hawaiian Island Concepts
P.O. Box 6280, Kahului, Maui, Hawaii 96732

Book design by Wagstaff Graphic Design, Maui, Hawaii.

Library of Congress Catalogue Card Number: #91-072018

ISBN #1-878498-02-9

Printed in Hong Kong.

THE SECRET
OF
THE HAWAIIAN
RAINBOW

A Hawaiian Story About Colors

Written by Stacey Kaopuiki   **Illustrated by Bob Wagstaff**

The Peter Panini Keiki Reader Series

There once was a time in Hawai'i when there were no rainbows. Whenever it rained, it was always dull, dark and gloomy.

A little **MENEHUNE** said, "Let us

make a **ĀNUENUE**, let us make a Hawaiian rainbow!"

So the **MENEHUNE** set out to find the very special colors that they would need.

'ULA'ULA

They took a red **KĀHILI** from the Royal Palace.

Red

'Ula'ula

Aka

'ALANI

They picked the soft, pretty orange flowers of the **'ILIMA**.

Orange

'Alani

Orenji

SQUEEZE
FIST

MELEMELE

They chose the ripest yellow **MAI'A** from the tallest banana trees near their village.

Yellow

Melemele

Kiiro

ŌMAʻOMAʻO

They gathered the many different
kinds of green ferns from
the mountains
and valleys.

Green

Ōma'oma'o

Midori

ULIULI

They filled an **'UMEKE** with clear, blue water taken from the deepest part of the sea.

Blue

Uliuli

Ao

Last of all, they snipped a small piece
of purple silk from the **HOLOKŪ**
of the Queen.

Purple

Poni

Murasaki

Then, the **MENEHUNE** placed all
that they had gathered into a large **KOA** bowl.

A **KAHUNA**, a Hawaiian wizard who had special powers and who was a friend of the **MENEHUNE**, then slowly began to mix and stir everything within the bowl.

When all the things they had gathered were blended together, the **KAHUNA** took a slender sugar cane flower stalk, dipped it into the bowl and held it up for all to see.

At the very tip of the cane stalk hung a tiny droplet of water.

Touched by the sunlight, the tiny droplet suddenly burst into all the colors that the **MENEHUNE** had gathered... all the colors of the Hawaiian Rainbow.

The **KAHUNA** then took his **KAKAKA**,
a small stick bow, and shot the cane stalk
like an arrow into a cloud.

A gentle rain began to fall.

"Into each raindrop is now stored
all the colors of the rainbow,"
said the **KAHUNA**.

The **MENEHUNE** began cheering.

Rainbows were appearing everywhere!

The sky was full of color.

The **KAHUNA** smiled and said,
"It will now be a sign to remind all people
of how important **WAI**, (water) and
UA (rain) is to all living things...
and its beauty will be
for all to enjoy."

GLOSSARY

'ALANI (ah-lah´-nee) Orange.

ĀNUENUE (ah-noo´-a-noo´-a) Rainbow.

HOLOKŪ (ho-lo-koo´) A long, formal flowing gown with a train.

'ILIMA (e-lee´-mah) Native shrub with orange or yellow flowers.

KĀHILI (kah-hee´-lee) A feathered staff, used as a symbol of Hawaiian royalty; comparable to a flag.

KAHUNA (kah-hoo´-nah) Hawaiian wizard, minister or master of any field.

KAKAKA (kah-kah-kah) A small bow.

KOA (koh´-ah) A large native tree whose high quality wood was used in many ways, especially in making canoes.

MAI'A (my´-ah) Banana.

MELEMELE (may´-lay-may´-lay) Yellow.

MENEHUNE (may´-nay-hoo´-nay) Legendary race of small people who worked at night building fish ponds, roads, temples; like Hawaiian elves.

ŌMA 'OMA 'O (o-mah´-o-mah´-o) Green.

PONI (poh´-nee) Purple.

UA (oo´-ah) Rain.

'ULA 'ULA (oo´-lah-oo´-lah) Red.

ULIULI (oo´-lee-oo´-lee) Blue.

'UMEKE (oo-may´-kay) Calabash, bowl made from a gourd or wood.

WAI (vai) Water, except sea water.